HATCHi

CROIRE AUX IDÉES, DONNER VIE AUX PROJETS

CONTENTS

1. INTRODUCTION

The Internet represents free access to unprecedented information. This network gives the possibility to anyone to access a quantity and a variety extraordinary information. It also gives anyone who wishes, the ability to publish information at any time and on a multitude of topics.

This exchange of information, continuously and in unlimited, brings us a progress undeniable but it also presents real difficulties for non-users experienced who would always like to stay at the top level in this field.

We have thought about and put in place a fun method that will allow you to simply understand how the Internet giants operate (Google, Amazon or Facebook ...) and thus stay at the forefront of the latest developments in terms Internet visibility.

Of course the tools evolve, but the basic method remains the same.

In this book we will describe Google's visibility and SEO, based on basic rules that can also be applied with others Internet giants.

I am Arnaud, co-founder of Agence Hatchi.
We offer customized training on customer acquisition and customer acquisition services on the Internet.
Despite a solid background at the Institut Mines-Telecom Business School and my experience in webmarketing within French and international startups, I have intially started in the digital without having any specific training at this field...

Surprising? Not really in the end...

We live in digitized world in which innovation is present at daily. What we know today can evolve or even be transformed into totality tomorrow.

Curiosity and learning ability (soft skills ... yes, it is) are qualities essential and much more important to succeed, than the skills acquired during a solid training (« hardskills »).

So, my expertise today is much more the result of my curiosity rather than my initial training... I take the paths that the Internet opens to find the latest trends : resources in English, French, free or premium.

I have the pleasure to share with you in this book what I learned, during my various digital.

Our goal is to show you that the use of this jargon appoints S.E.O (Search Engine Optimization) is in fact not only intended for experts, but also to you !

HATCHI SAS - RCS Bordeaux B 841 624 083
arnaud@agencehatchi.fr
HATCHI SAS – All Rights Reserved

This machine is Google, actually works in the same way as us, humans. I would dare to call this ROBOT HUMAN - 😊

Scary? No, because you will understand how it works and so how better to appropriate it.

Before starting, I insist that curiosity and the desire to learn are the essential qualities that you must possess to live happily in this digitized world.

Good news, you already have them since you are reading this book!

We will start by studying how Google works by comparing it to real estate agency.

We will then see 4 perfectly human and comprehensible aspects on which Google (and other giants of the WEB), rely to place our content web at the forefront.

We will finally be interested in the latest trends in 2019 with tips that you can apply to optimize your digital strategy.

IN SHORT
The qualities to succeed in the digital world in 2019:

1. Curiosity

2. Learning ability

--> you already have them because you are reading this book!

HATCHI SAS - RCS Bordeaux B 841 624 083
arnaud@agencehatchi.fr
HATCHI SAS – All Rights Reserved

2. THE REAL ESTATE AGENCY

« Google's mission is « to organize information globally and to make it universally accessible and useful » » – Wikipedia

Google, as you certainly know is a tool that allows Internet users to find the information they are looking for.

  a) The user types a query or question on Google based on keywords
  b) Google interprets the keywords of the user's query
  c) Then Google decides to display first the websites that it interprets as best answering the user's query or question

Thus, the goal of Google is to help the user to find the web page (information) which best suits his needs (his initial query based on the keywords) among all the web pages he knows about (the web pages "indexed" by Google, for our purist friends).

I often compare Google to a real estate agency ...

Why ?

The objective of the real estate agency is to find the property that meets the better to the customer's need.

So :

  a) The client will see the real estate agency and transmit its search criteria. Ex: « I would like a house in San Francisco which is 100m², with three bedrooms, a swimming pool and a budget of 800 000 dollars. »

  b) The real estate agency then retains the criteria « House », « San Francisco », « 100m² », « Three rooms », « swimming pool » and « 800,000 dollars ».

  c) Then the real estate agency searches its database (where all its real estate are registered) to offer the client, the property which best fits his criteria.

  d) And finally the customer is satisfied and the real estate agent too because he can benefit a nice little commission ...

Google works the same way !

a) The user researches on Google « house San Francisco 100 m² with 3 rooms a pool and a budget of 800,000 dollars ».

b) Google retains the search criteria of the user that are not other than the keywords.

c) Google interprets the query by « What is the best house available in San Francisco which is 100m ² with 3 bedrooms, a pool and for a purchase price 800,000 dollars ? »

d) Google looks in its entire database to see which web pages best match the user's criteria (which correspond to the better to the retained keywords).

e) Then Google offers the customer a list of web pages that correspond to criteria - the websites posted on Google are actually called web pages "because they make up the websites. Google will first display the pages that it deems best to match the research.

☺ The only difference being that he does not receive commission as real estate agent: the tool offers a 100% free service to the user.

IN SHORT
1. The client will see the real estate agent with his request:
"I want to buy a house of 150m² in San Francisco, I have a budget of 800000 dollars"

2. The real estate agent looks among his offers and offers the one that best meets the customer criteria

HATCHI SAS - RCS Bordeaux B 841 624 083
arnaud@agencehatchi.fr
HATCHI SAS – All Rights Reserved

1. The customer is searching on Google:

house 150 m2 san francisco 800000 dollars

Google Search   I'm Feeling Lucky

2. Google looks through the websites and first
displays the one that best meets the
customer criteria

3. UNDERSTANDING SEO IN 4 EASY STEPS

Now that you better understand how Google works (or any other search engine), we can look at this famous question:

How does Google decide to display a website first compared to others?

Before answering this question, let's not forget this:

a) The main purpose of Google is to display to the user, **information** that **best** corresponds to his need, expressed need through the searched **keywords**.

b) Thus, each user search is interpreted by Google by a **question**: « What is the best, the best » + the keywords that are the criteria of the request.
Do you remember:
« What is the best house available in Arcachon which is 100m² with 3 rooms, a pool and for a purchase price of 800,000 dollars? »

Subsequently, I consider the user search as a question because it is this way that Google interprets it.

c) So, once the user expresses his request and Google interprets it **question**, Google should classify this long list of websites (web pages), to display his best **answer to the question: the website-answer that best meets the user's request.**

HATCHI SAS - RCS Bordeaux B 841 624 083
arnaud@agencehatchi.fr
HATCHI SAS – All Rights Reserved

Let's position ourselves in this question-answer process:

- the question is asked by the user (Google interprets it this way) and the answer is expressed by the website.
- Google's mission is to find this answer and show it to the user.

To answer the user's question, Google is based on 4 criteria chronological easy to understand for us humans:

1. Understanding the answers
2. Analysis of the content of the answers
3. The wording of the answers
4. Confidence in these answers

1. Understanding the answers

Generally speaking, when asking a question, we expect understand the potential answers so that you can then know which answers the best to the question.
(Ex: If you are asking a question in French, you are expecting certainly to an answer in French.)
Once the user has asked his question, Google will search among the different websites to determine if the answer is there.
He must therefore be able to understand the content of the website (the content of the potential answer) to determine whether it can be displayed or not.

The website must therefore express its content in the same language as Google in order to be easily understood by Google.

- There is French, English, Chinese ... And the WEB language which is universal!

- This is the grammar to use, different rules to follow for« Speak » the Internet language.

- Grammar rules are the tags that you can see in the code of a website: You can do the test by going to your favorite website, right click then click on « show the source code of the page » and you will see the code of the site with the tags such as « <html class = », « <head> » etc ... which communicates to Google the content of the site.

HATCHI SAS - RCS Bordeaux B 841 624 083
arnaud@agencehatchi.fr
HATCHI SAS – All Rights Reserved

Once these rules are applied correctly, Google can understand the website and analyze its content to determine if it can potentially answer the user's question.

IN SHORT

There is French, English, Chinese ...

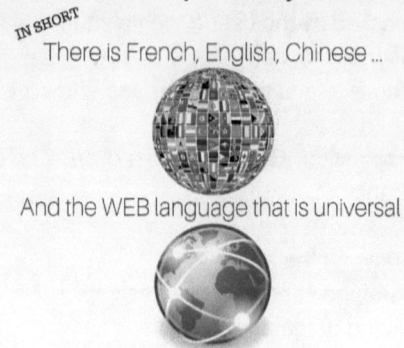

And the WEB language that is universal

2. Analysis of the content of the answers

Once we are sure that our interlocutors speak the same language that we want to make sure they do not respond off-topic to our question, is not it?

Well, Google proceeds in the same way as us.

The tool (Google) will then read the content of the website page to detect similarities between his potential answer and the user search.
Google is then based on the consistency between the **keywords** present in the question of the internet user and the **keywords** that are present in the website.

- If the same keywords exist in the tags of the web page, it will be then retained by Google (do you remember these tags in the preceding paragraph, which symbolize the grammatical rules to be followed to allow Google to understand the web page?).

- In the last part of this book, we will see the exhaustive list of grammar rules to respect to allow Google to understand easily the content of the web pages.

So to summarize, Google makes sure that the words-used by the user are clearly visible in the content of the web page:

→ the web page will not be off-topic in relation to the question of the user.

HATCHI SAS - RCS Bordeaux B 841 624 083
arnaud@agencehatchi.fr
HATCHI SAS – All Rights Reserved

3. The wording of the answers

The website meets the two previous criteria:
- o It is understood, therefore detectable by Google.
- o It can potentially answer the user's question because its content contains the keywords of his question.

Let's continue to place ourselves in this analogy to the question / answer. Imagine asking the same question to different people.

- What do you prefer from the choices below?

    - o The response of a person, which is expressed correctly and politely with extra, enriching information on the theme of your question?

    - o Or the response of a person, expressed with mistakes of languages, which can lead to misinterpretation?

At first, you prefer the first type of answer. Logic!

And well Google behaves the same way to measure this third criterion.

The tool will consider an important parameter in the world of the web: the user experience.

Thus, Google is able to detect:

- A web page that provides a **good « user experience »**:
  when a user stays on a web page (this shows that the user **is interested** in the content of the page)

- A web page that provices a **bad « user experience »**:
  when a user immediatly leaves the web page, closing it by example (this shows that the user **is not interested** in the content of the page)

The web page is attractive
→ the wording of the web page is good
→ the user stays on the web page
→ the wording of the answer is good

So we could ask ourselves what to do to keep the user on the web page ?

Here are the most important criteria to allow the user to stay on the web page and therefore to transmit a good user experience.

<u>The web page must offer quality content:</u>

- It is displayed **quickly**, as well on **smartphone, tablet or computer**.

- **Original** content (no copy and paste from another website).

- Content that provides **solutions** and **answers** to the user at his initial question (the searched keywords).

- Content that **enriches** the user's knowledge by providing them with **additional information** in relation to the subject of his question.
For example, a user who is initially looking for hotels will be happy to see on the site of a hotel: ideas of traditional restaurants, activities to do during his stay.

- **Entertaining** content including **photos** and **videos**.

So the answer provided by the website, to the initial question of the user (the search for the user) is well formulated.

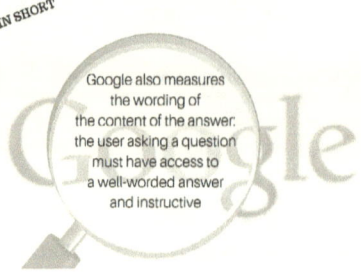

This leads us to the ultimate criterion for placing or not placing a website at the top of the pages displayed by Google.

HATCHI SAS - RCS Bordeaux B 841 624 083
arnaud@agencehatchi.fr
HATCHI SAS – All Rights Reserved

4. Confidence in the answer

If you ask a question about a particular topic to two people, one of them being rather novice while the other is expert in this area ...

Which   answer   will   you   favor?   That   of   the   expert!

If we have the choice between several answers or several website, we always choose the one with the highest level of expertise on the subject. The answer / website then brings confidence to the topic.

Like us humans, Google values experts: those who generate trust on a subject.

Here are some examples that illustrate the expertise of an answer to a question – so the expertise of a website in search of the user:

- o The website (the answer) uses the secure connection « https »
  → security = trust

    🔒 https://www.wikipedia.org

- o The answer is already generating a lot of **positive feedback** from users satisfied.

- o The answer is quoted in the content of other websites like **reference** on the subject.

- o The answer quotes **expert sources** for argumentation.
  Ex: a hotel website that offers links to the websites of best restaurants in the city.

- o So how do you generate Google's trust and maximize its chances to appear among the first websites posted by this one.

IN SHORT

Do you prefer the answer of an expert
to that of an amateur?
Google too!

HATCHI SAS - RCS Bordeaux B 841 624 083
arnaud@agencehatchi.fr
HATCHI SAS – All Rights Reserved

To sum up, Google and search engines in general work this way:

1. The user searches by typing keywords
   Ex: « Hotel Hawaii »

2. The search engine interprets the search with a question
   Ex: « Which is the best hotel in Hawaii? »

3. The search engine will try to display to the user the answers to his question (websites) - by classifying the list of answers in order to to post in 1st position the best answer to the question

4. The search engine is based on the classification criteria following:

   a. Understanding the answer - speak the same language as the search engine → so that the search engine can read the content of the answer

   b. The content of the answer - the similarities between the keywords
      searched by the users and the keywords contained in the answer → so that the user can find his answer

   c. The formulation of the answer → so that the user can spend an enriching moment by learning about the answer to his question

   d. Trust in the answer → so that the user can access an expert response, in a secure way

4. SEO IN 2019 : TIPS AND PRACTICES

Now that we understand how search engines work, we are able to understand the tips and best practices below, that can optimize the rank of his site on Google (for example).

a) The detailed actions to be carried out to achieve each good practice are in below the table on the next page.

b) I have voluntarily classified the various good practices to be place following the factors **difficulty**, **time** and **money**.
Knowing that most of these good practices are free.

→ first are the fastest and least good practices demanding in terms of skills

c) Indeed, we do not all benefit from the same resources for set up a digital strategy!

d) We will see in this table at which stage of analysis each action corresponds – I refer to the criteria previously seen: understanding, content, wording or confidence in the answer.

HATCHI SAS - RCS Bordeaux B 841 624 083
arnaud@agencehatchi.fr
HATCHI SAS – All Rights Reserved

Good Practice	Why realize or visualize it (It corresponds at what criterion of analysis)	Competency or prerequisite to attain one's goals (Level of difficulty to attain or achieve goals)	Necessary time to complete it (Average estimation which can vary)	Cost
To possess a good reputation on Google map	To increase the confidence in the enterprise	No competencies. But it is necessary to possess some photos of the enterprise or of the product.	1. 30 minutes to create an account on Google My Business 2. To wait 3-5 days to receive the verification courier from Google 3. To fill the profile of the enterprise on Google Map - 30 minutes 4. To ask for notes and advice - 10 minutes each day for 2 weeks to attain a positive reputation	Free
To determine the needs of the clients by use of Google tools for the best response in the contained website	To propose an answer adapted to the user's question	No specific competency.	1. 60 minutes for the first usage 2. 20 minutes for the second usage etc....	Free
To ensure the secured connection of the website	To increase the confidence in the enterprise	No specific competency.	30 minutes	From 20 dollars / year
To know the questions of the potential clients by use of the tool "answerthepublic"	To formulate positive user experience : to know the clients needs for the best responses	No specific competency.	20 minutes	Free for basic usage
To speak the language Google	To publish a web content which is easily understood and analysed by Google	To have some notions or ideas of web development, SEO and web wording or redaction	30 minutes to optimize an 800 word article	Free
To control the global SEO of one's website by use of the tool SEOquake	To assure that the 4 aspects: Comprehension, Contents, Formulation, and Confidence, are followed well	To have some advanced foundation in SEO	30 minutes for the first usage and global comprehension It is possible then to use the tool in the manner that is the most expedient.	Free

Good practice N°1

Have a good reputation on Google Map

a. Register your business on Google My Business
b. Update your company profile
c. Ask top customers to rate and review Google Maps
d. No customers yet?
   Ask friends / family who believe in the business to rate and review on Google Map.

Good practice N°2

-> The actions are voluntarily detailed because it is a powerful tool and which requires a Google Ads account (free to create):

Determine the need of customers to better meet them in the content of the website

a. To vaguely define your position:

   Answer the question: « What do I propose to my clients? »
   Define, in a maximum of ten words, what you sell, your activity or your services:

   (Ex: « real estate agency in San Francisco, sale and purchase of house ».)

b. Access the tool that will show what your customers are looking for

   Find out what your future customers are looking for on the Internet with the help of Google, « the keyword planning tool » - which will be called afterwards « **Keyword Planner** » :

   Depending on your geographic targeting, you can find out what you're looking for
   exactly your future customers on the Internet!

You need to have a Google Ads account (free) to access this tool, here are the easy steps to follow:

i. Type on Google « Adwords keywords planner » and access the Keywords planner website

ii. Then, at the bottom left, right below « Reach the right customers with the right keywords. » :

    1. Click   on   « Access   the   Keyword   Planner »

START USING KEYWORD PLANNER ➡

If you have a Google Account then sign in via your Google Account - and you can go directly to step « iii », below after substep « 4 ».

Or, if you do not have a Google Account yet, continue with step « 2 » below.

    2. Follow the account creation steps up to what your Google Account is created.

(Ps): you can enter the surname, first name, date of birth

HATCHI SAS - RCS Bordeaux B 841 624 083
arnaud@agencehatchi.fr
HATCHI SAS – All Rights Reserved

3. Next, accept and validate the conditions after having unfolded the menu down.

Privacy and Terms

that we use across all of our services.

You're in control
Depending on your account settings, some of this data may be associated with your Google Account and we treat this data as personal information. You can control how we collect and use this data now by clicking 'More Options' below. You can always adjust your controls later or withdraw your consent for the future by visiting My Account (myaccount.google.com).

MORE OPTIONS ⌄

☑ I agree to the Google Terms of Service

☑ I agree to the processing of my information as described above and further explained in the Privacy Policy

Cancel   **Create Account**

iii. You can now create your free Google Ads account

1. Click on « Do you already know Google Ads? »

2. Then, click on "Create an account without a campaign"

3. And finally click on « Send » (this validation will have no incidence):

iv. Congratulations, you have created your Google Ads account!

NB : it is a very useful tool to promote your activity or your product on the Internet in the whole world.

This is one of the tools we use at the HATCHI Agency to make our customers win clients.

c. Use the tool to find out what your future customers are looking for on Google

    i. Click on the top right on:

    ii. Then, at the top left:

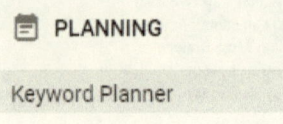

    iii. And, click on:

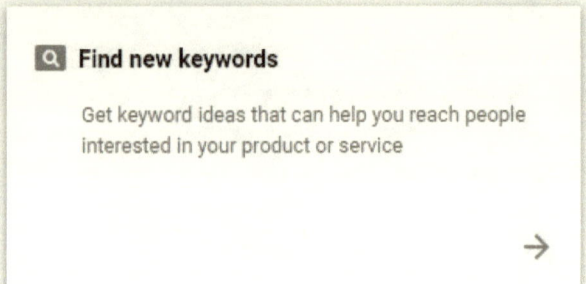

This will allow you to know the exact searches of your potential customers on Google.

    iv. Finally, put yourself in the shoes of your potential customers and write this that they could look for - in our example « buying house san francisco »:

       1. Then click on:

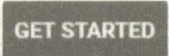

    v. Congratulations, you now have access to the research of your potential customers on Google!

You can appreciate the exact searches of your potential customers.

PS: If there are many results posted, very good !
This means there are a lot of potential customers 👍.

d. Learn how to interpret the result displayed by Google

   i.   How to interpret and modify the geographic targeting?
Geographical targeting:

Geographical targeting: where potential customers are connected to who you want to sell your product / service.

As you can see below, targeting is default « France » - all of France, so not a lot of results in this case.

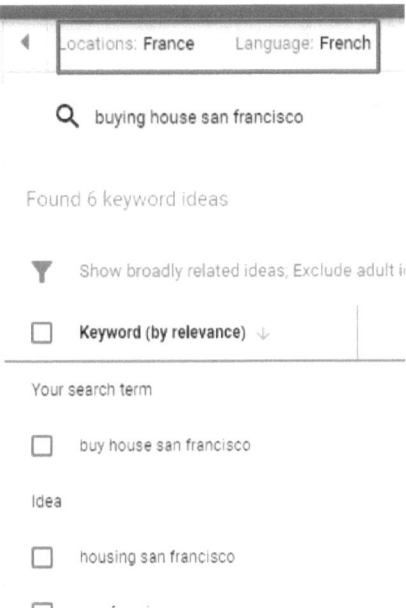

   ii.   Click on « Locations » and update with for instance « United States » and click on « Save »:

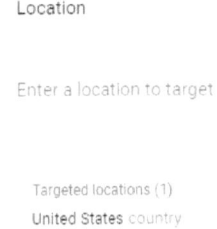

You can click on « Language » and update it to english it may bring more results in our case :

Language: French ✏

iii. If you do not want to target everyone who lives in US, you can refine or modify the geographical location by clicking on the cross.

Then you can indicate the place you want to target, by writing the name of   the place (ex: California)):

1. Click the name of your targeting when it appears.

2. Then, at the bottom right, click

The results now show all the searches of your potential customers in California → you can orient your Internet content according to the keywords you choose.

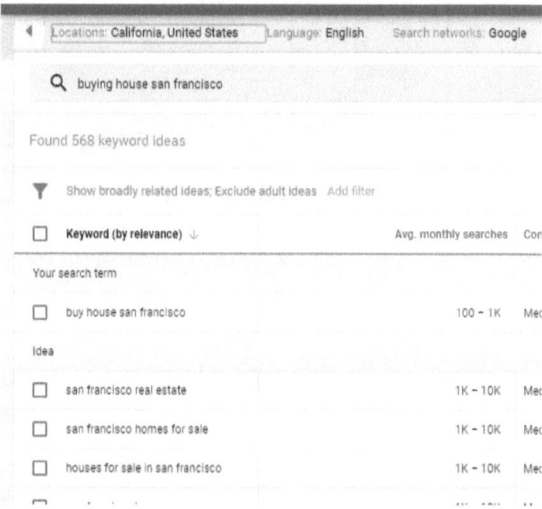

3. You can change your geo-targeting again if need, repeating the action just described.

NB : as you will see, this too has no limit – you can find out what searches for a person according to their geographical location and language everywhere in the world…

HATCHI SAS - RCS Bordeaux B 841 624 083
arnaud@agencehatchi.fr
HATCHI SAS – All Rights Reserved

Good practice N° 3:

Ensure the secure connection of the website:

    a. Go to your domain name provider's website
       (domain name = website name)

    b. Or on websites such as :
       https://www.cloudflare.com/

    c. Then follow the necessary steps - buy the SSL certificate that suits you - each SSL certificate gives you a secure connection, which is the most important

Good practice N° 4:

Speak the Google language

Once you have understood the good practice 2, you can choose your keywords to create web content that meets the customer's needs.

To be visible and understood by Google quickly, make sure your keywords are listed in   the locations below, the list is exhaustive, it is not imperative to apply everything but it is preferable:

- **title – title of the web page** - visible in the red box below:

    1. Wikipedia
       https://www.wikipedia.org/ ▾
       Wikipedia is a free online encyclopedia
       hosted by the Wikimedia Foundation.

- **URL – the web address of the web page** - visible in the red box below:

- **meta description – the description of the content of the web page –** visible on the red box below:

1. Wikipedia

https://www.wikipedia.org/ ▾

Wikipedia is a free online encyclopedia, created and edited by volunteers around the world and hosted by the Wikimedia Foundation.

- **headline – the title of the content of the web page** - visible in the red box below in the top left corner:

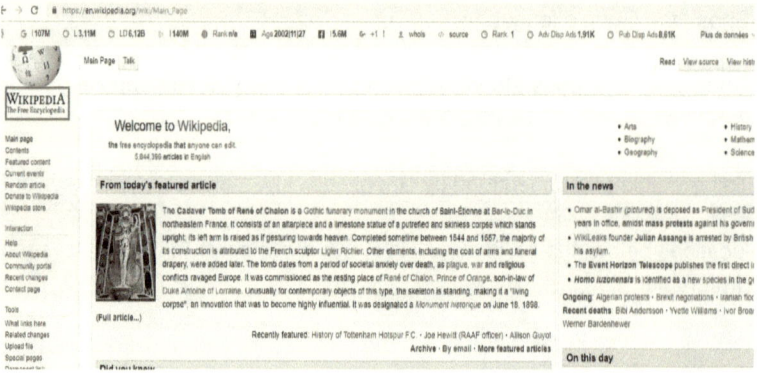

- At least **in 1 of the subtitles** - the subtitle of the content of the web page - visible in the red boxes below (in this case it would have been necessary to see the Wikipedia's name to be totally detectable by Google - but still a once we consider the « perfect » case that is different from most cases):

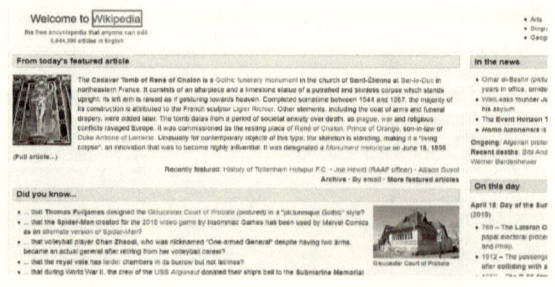

HATCHI SAS - RCS Bordeaux B 841 624 083
arnaud@agencehatchi.fr
HATCHI SAS – All Rights Reserved

- In the **1st paragraph** of the content of the web page

- At the **end of the content** of the web page

- **Naturally over the content** of the web page

- **alt image. tag** – which is the tag of an image or video that is in the web page

- **Title and description of the name of the image or video** – at the time of setting update of the image on the website: For example, if you add an image, name it: « your_keyword_choice.jpg »

Good practice N°5:

Know the questions of potential customers

a. Go to the website: https://answerthepublic.com/ - do not trust the gentleman strange with his glasses 😑

b. Scroll down to search bar - red box below:

c. Enter then keywords that your customers are likely to search below « Enter your keyword ... » but stay vague - ex: « hotels » then select « Get Questions »

d. And then appears below the set of questions that potential customers arise in relation to the keywords!

<u>Good practice N°6 :</u>

Ensure that the **4 aspects**: understanding, content, wording and trust are well followed.

a. Download Google Chrome, if it is not yet downloaded to your computer

b. Through Google Chrome, go to https://www.seoquake.com/index.html

c. Click on « Add it as an extension »

d. Follow the steps to add the extension - then the SEO quake logo should appear at the top right of Google Chrome:

e. Go to the web page you choose

f. Right click

g. Then click like this - Seoquake and Diagnosis

h. Finally, the audit and tips to improve the web page appear!

We live in a digital world in which innovation is daily: what we know today can be refined or transformed tomorrow.

However, the Internet represents free access to unprecedented information.

Our curiosity and learning ability are our best allies to live happily in this digitized world!

And to go further, the Agency HATCHI offers services and personalized digital training on **customer acquisition**

Do not hesitate to contact us, we will be happy to meet your expectations: arnaud@agencehatchi.fr.

Hoping to have aroused your curiosity and nourished your hunger for knowledge, we wish you every success in your 2019 digital strategy!

HATCHi

CROIRE AUX IDÉES, DONNER VIE AUX PROJETS

HATCHI SAS - RCS Bordeaux B 841 624 083
arnaud@agencehatchi.fr
HATCHI SAS – All Rights Reserved

www.ingramcontent.com/pod-product-compliance
Lightning Source LLC
Chambersburg PA
CBHW031942170526
45157CB00008B/3280

* 9 7 8 1 0 9 5 9 8 9 2 4 1 *